HOW TO
read
drum music

STU SEGAL & JIMMY SICA

LIBERTY PUBLISHING
METUCHEN, NEW JERSEY, USA

First Printing 2012
Second Printing 2013
Third Printing 2014
Fourth Printing 2017

To our parents, whose love of music fostered our own,
and to Peggy and Rashmika,
without whom none of this would be possible.

ACKNOWLEDGEMENTS

Cover Design by Stephen H. Segal

Thanks to Matt Patella for his input.

Thanks to Chad Criswell and MusicEdMagic.com
for his arrangement of Yankee Doodle.

And a big Thank You! to our "beta testers":
Vanessa Ellis
Rashmika Segal
Pete Yachimovicz

CONTENTS

INTRODUCTION

What You Will Get Out of Reading Drum Music

It is likely you fall into one of two categories—either you are not a musician, have never read music, and have decided to learn to play drums . . . or, you *are* a musician, have learned to play, but have never been taught to read music. Either way, this book will benefit you greatly.

If you are completely new to playing drums, reading music will open up the magical world of playing music. You probably love music, which is why you want to play. Well, every piece of music you've ever heard can be written, and most of it has. Being able to read the music is the key that unlocks the playing.

Now this is not to say that because you are able to read and understand the notes on paper you'll necessarily be able to perform them; just like all great musicians you'll need to develop and perfect proper technique. But the starting point of it all is the ability to read. The ability to read, and then to practice, the techniques that will form the basis of your playing. The ability to read and understand the genres and pieces of music you want to perform. Reading . . . it's the cornerstone of your musical education.

Suppose though you already play, but can't read. First of all, if you've bought this book you have already identified your own need to be able to read; there could be any number of reasons. First, and most obvious, you've heard other drummers perform patterns and sounds that you just haven't been able to figure out, and you know if you could read you could see the exact way to perform what you've heard. Second, perhaps you recently saw an ad for a job in an off-Broadway show, as I once did, and it read: "Must be able to juggle, play an instrument, read music and perform stand-up comedy." (I could do the hard stuff, but guess what – I couldn't read music, so I couldn't even apply.)

So perhaps you want to read to enter the world of music, perhaps you already play and want to improve, or maybe you even want to pursue a career as a professional musician. Reading music will open the door, and will provide you as much enjoyment and benefit as reading English.

Drum Music is Not Like Other Music

Generally when folks think about reading music, they envision "notes"—meaning they think each note represents a certain tone or "pitch". An A, a C, a G, and so on. And if you were playing a flute or a saxophone this would be true; each note would represent a specific tone that is to be played. If you were playing a guitar, piano, or other stringed or keyboard instrument there would also be "chords", which are combinations of notes that are to be played simultaneously. With the exception of drums, instruments create notes which are a high pitch, or a low pitch, and are therefore "pitched instruments".

Drums are not "pitched". A drum makes basically the same sound each time you strike it, though it may be louder or softer depending how hard you strike. So for drumming, though the notes may look the same as for other instruments, they do not represent the same thing.[1]

In drum music, each note will tell you when to strike the instrument. The note may tell you whether to accent by striking hard, or to strike softly. The note will tell you which instrument to strike—it may be the snare, the tom, the bass, one of your cymbals, or the hi-hat. The notes will tell you when to play quickly, or slowly. So drum music is all about what you are striking, when, and how hard.

Reading Music, Versus Reading Drum Tabs

Perhaps you've seen "tabs". You can find drum tabs for some popular songs, and you can also find guitar and bass tabs. Tabs are a form of musical notation for folks who don't read music.

Tabs are generally a series of x's and o's, placed amid dashes. The x's and o's tell you when to play. In the example below the CC line is crash cymbal, HH is hi-hat, SN is snare and BA is bass.

```
CC | X--------------- | ----------------- | ----------------- | ----------------- |
HH | x---x---x---x--- | x---x---x---x--- | x---x---x---x--- | x---x---x---x--- |
SN | ----o-------o--- | ----o-------o--- | ----o-------o--- | ----o-------o--- |
BA | o-------o------- | o-------o------- | o-------o------- | o-------o------- |
```

This is an excerpt from a longer piece, and the instructions are to play at 135 beats per minute. As you can see, you are supposed to strike each instrument according to the tab—on the first note you would strike the Crash Cymbal, Hi-hat and Bass simultaneously, on the next the Hi-hat and the Snare, on the next the Hi-hat and the Bass, and so on.

Interestingly, when you look carefully at how drum tabs are written, it is similar to the traditional way that music is written; it tells you what notes to play, and when. But it lacks the framework which allows written music to add both more information and nuance—and let's be clear, the depth and color of written music, versus tabs, is like the difference between Beethoven's 5th Symphony and a jingle for a TV commercial.

There are two problems with tabs. The first and most obvious is the system is intentionally simplistic, and as a result tabs can't properly communicate complex moves, figures and rhythms. The second, and not so obvious, is that learning to read music is not very much more difficult than learning tabs, and the advantage is enormous.

---

[1] There *are* pitched percussion instruments. Xylophone, glockenspiel, vibraphones are all percussion instruments that produce notes of various pitches. Music notation for these pitched percussion instruments is more akin to music for pitched instruments than it is to drums.

It would be similar to learning just the most often used letters of the English language, which would limit you to learning only the words that use those letters—versus learning all the letters and having access to all the words in our language.

Our assessment is—why spend the time to learning drum tabs and limit yourself? Put the same effort into learning traditional notation and you will have no limits.

Why We've Written This Book

There are two reasons:

First, we've looked everywhere, and we can't find a single book on how to read drum music. Yes, there are books on reading music, but not drum music. Yes, there are many books on how to *play* drums. And yes, there are tons of websites about playing drums, and learning drums. But these sites all assume you already know how to read drum music, or you don't care to learn.

The second reason is more personal. We have both enjoyed the benefits, both personal and professional, of reading drum music—we would love to know that we helped you learn too.

HOW TO
read
drum music

How to Use This Book

A few suggestions to help you get the most out of this book.

- Start in the beginning and **do the book in order**. The things you learn on the early pages are required for the later pages. Learning to read music is like any other learning process—the basics come first.

- Each example is explained on a left page, and the musical notation appears on the facing right page. **Thoroughly read** the explanation on the left page, and refer to the facing notation.

- **Set up a practice pad and tap out what you're reading.**

- Many of the individual examples in the book are demonstrated on videos at our website. For those examples, read the text, **watch the video**, then do the exercise yourself. Examples which are demonstrated on video are labeled on the bottom of the page:

For the video, go to our website,
www.drummerSS.com

- **Count the notes out loud**. It will help you with proper placement of the notes.

Do us a favor, please!
If you enjoy our book, if it teaches you to read drum music, gives you a better understanding of written music, teaches you about time signatures, please help us get the book out to others. Please go to amazon.com and rate our book! It'll just take a minute.
Thank you!

The Framework Within Which Music is Written

Music is written on a background which is called a *staff*. The staff is comprised of five horizontal lines on which the notes are placed. The space between two vertical lines is called a "bar", or a "measure".

Music which is written for pitched instruments uses the vertical placement of each note on the staff to signify what pitch is to be played—this is not true for drums. For drums, the vertical placement on the staff indicates which *instrument* is to be struck.

Generally, written drum music will show, from the top of the staff to the bottom[2]:

        Crash Cymbal
        Hi-hat played with stick
        Ride Cymbal
        High Tom Tom
        Middle Tom Tom
        Snare Drum
        Floor Tom Tom
        Bass Drum
        Hi-hat played with foot

---

[2] It is possible (though not likely) that placement of instruments on the staff could differ from the example above, based on the preference of the composer. It is also possible other percussion instruments could be shown. In either of those cases, the composer will provide a key or a notation.

What Notes Look Like

First measure ⇨
   We have a whole note. It looks like a squashed O. The whole note means that there is only one, single note played in the measure. *A measure can contain only one whole note, or any division of that whole note, as you will see below.*

Second measure ⇨
   Two half notes. The two half notes are played in the same timeframe as the whole note, but two notes are played.

Third measure ⇨
   Further dividing up the notes. Four quarter notes can be played in the same space as one whole note, or two half notes.

Fourth measure ⇨
   Now we divide the measure up into eight eighth notes. Notice that the eighth notes can be joined together with one "beam" across the top of the notes, or they can appear as single notes, with a little flag waving to the right.

Fifth measure ⇨
   Sixteenth notes. Again, sixteenth notes can be beamed across the top, but with *two* beams, or can be written as single notes, with two flags.

Sixth measure ⇨
   Thirty-second notes. And thirty-second notes will appear with three beams or flags.

Example 1 – What Notes Look Like

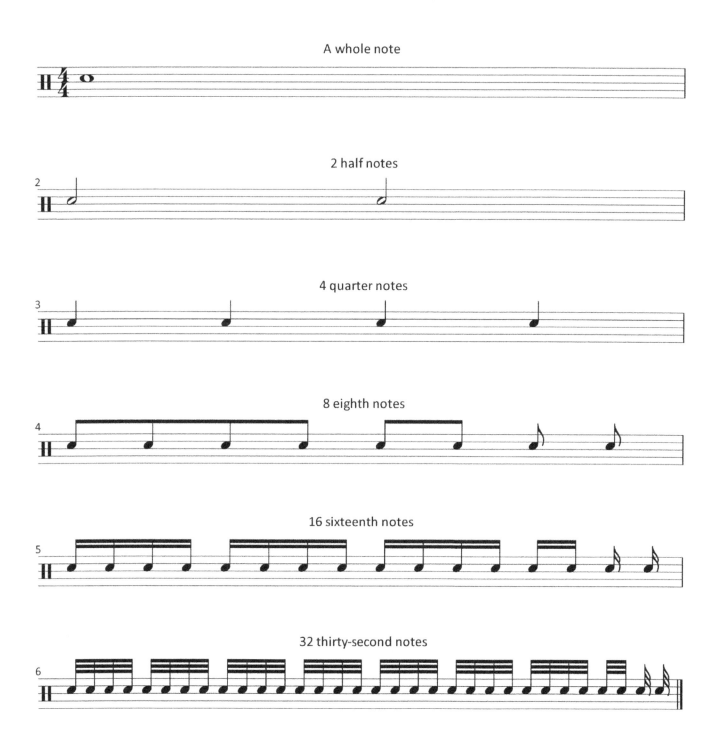

What Rests Look Like

Every measure is not completely filled with notes. Sometimes there is a note, and sometimes there is not—when there is not a note there is a rest. When there is a rest, you do just that, you rest; you do not play anything.

First measure ⇨

    A whole note rest. This means you rest for the duration of a whole note, which is a whole measure. Or another way to say it is . . . when you see a whole note rest, you play nothing in that measure.

Second measure ⇨

    A half note, and a half note rest. You would play the first half note, and rest (not play) the second.

Third measure ⇨

    3 quarter notes, and a quarter note rest. Again, you would play the first 3 quarter notes, and rest (not play) the fourth.

Measures 4, 5 and 6 ⇨

    And so on . . . eighth notes, sixteenth notes and thirty-second notes. In every example you would play the notes and rest (not play) where the rests are shown

Example 2 – What Rests Look Like

The Time Signature

At the beginning of every piece of music you will see what looks like a fraction, 3/4 or 4/4 or perhaps 6/8, or something else. It is not a fraction, it is the "time signature" of the composition.

The time signature tells you how many beats there are in each measure, and the duration of each beat. (We divide music into "beats"; the "beat" is the pulse of the music.) The top number tells you how many beats per measure, and the bottom number tells you the length of each beat.

Let us consider 4/4 time. The top number tells us there are 4 beats per measure, and the bottom number tells us that each beat is a quarter note long. That means there are four quarter notes, *or any combination which equals four quarter notes*, in the measure—for instance, there could be 3 quarter notes, and two eighth notes (since two eighth notes equal a quarter note), or any other combination equal to four quarter notes.

Let us look at the example below. The time signature, 4/4, appears at the beginning.

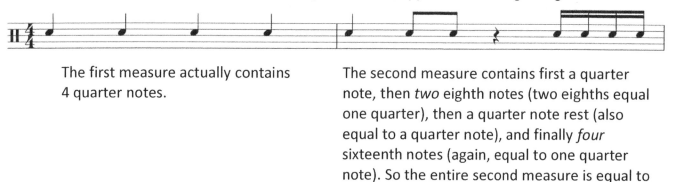

The first measure actually contains 4 quarter notes.

The second measure contains first a quarter note, then *two* eighth notes (two eighths equal one quarter), then a quarter note rest (also equal to a quarter note), and finally *four* sixteenth notes (again, equal to one quarter note). So the entire second measure is equal to 4 quarter notes.

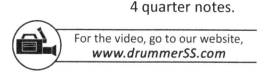

For the video, go to our website,
www.drummerSS.com

For the purpose of this book, we will keep nearly everything in 4/4 time. You will however see other time signatures on other pieces of music—remember, the top number tells you how many beats in a measure. The bottom number tells you the duration of each beat; if the bottom number is a 4 then each beat is a quarter note, if the bottom number is an 8 then each beat is an eighth note. So if you see a 6/8 time signature, you will know that there are 6 beats in each measure, and each beat is an eighth note (or any combination which equals an eighth note) long.[3]

---

[3] There are also 2 symbols that are sometimes used as time signatures:
   When **C** appears as the time signature it is called "common time", and is the same as 4/4.
   When **¢** appears as the time signature it is called "cut time", and is the same as 4/4 *except* everything is cut in half; whole notes become half notes, half notes become quarter notes, etc.

How to Count Notes

Let's start with *why* it is important to count the notes. You will see notes written on paper—somehow you need translate these notes for your brain to process—and what your brain understands is language. So what you need to do is convert those notes on paper into a language your brain understands, and do so in a way that lets you play the right notes at the right time.

First measure ⇨
>   There are four quarter notes. The count is, simply:

1   2   3   4

Second measure ⇨
>   This measure shows eighth notes, which are counted:

1 AN 2 AN 3 AN 4 AN

Third measure ⇨
>   We have sixteenth notes. The way you will count sixteenth notes is:

1 E AN DA 2 E AN DA 3 E AN DA 4 E AN DA

Fourth measure ⇨
>   Quarter notes again . . . *but,* now that we know how to count sixteenth notes, we are going to use the sixteenth note count (just as we used in the third measure) to count the quarter notes. This will help us properly space the quarter notes across the measure:

1 E AN DA **2** E AN DA **3** E AN DA **4** E AN DA

Fifth measure ⇨
>   Eighth notes. Again, we will use the sixteenth note count to help us properly space these notes:

1 E **AN** DA **2** E **AN** DA **3** E **AN** DA **4** E **AN** DA

Example 3 – How to Count Notes in 4/4 Time

If everything were written in whole notes, half notes and quarter notes, as on the following page, then you would count everything in quarter notes . . . that is, 1 2 3 4.

Measures 1 and 2 ⇨

So in Measure 1 you would play the whole note on the count of 1, then nothing on 2, 3, 4.
In Measure 2, which contains a whole note rest, you would count 1, 2, 3, 4 and play nothing.

Measures 3 and 4 ⇨

In Measure 3 which contains 2 half notes, you would play on the count of 1, nothing on the 2, play on 3, nothing on 4. Measure 4 contains a half note rest, followed by a half note—so you would rest on 1 and 2, play on 3, nothing on 4.

Measures 5 and 6 ⇨

In Measure 5 we have 4 quarter notes, so you would play on the counts of 1, 2, 3 and 4. Measure 6 contains a rest on the last quarter note, so you would play on 1, 2, 3, rest on 4.

Measures 7 and 8 ⇨

Measure 7, play on 1 , 2, rest on 3, play on 4. Measure 8, play on 1, rest on 2, play on 3 , 4.

Measures 9 through 12 ⇨

Measure 9, rest on 1, play on 2, 3, 4. In measures 10, 11 and 12 we have a mix of whole notes, half notes and quarter notes, and to avoid confusion, you will count everything as quarter notes.

Example 4 – Whole, Half, Quarter Notes and Rests

Now we're going to look at a page that contains eighth notes—remembering of course, that two eighth notes fit in the same space as one quarter note—and we're going to count everything as eighth notes:

1   AN   2   AN   3   AN   4   AN

Measures 1 and 2 ⇨

In Measure 1 you would play the quarter notes on 1, 2, 3, 4. Same thing in Measure 2, but as we see a rest on the 4th beat you would play only 1, 2, 3, and rest on 4.

Measures 3 and 4 ⇨

Measure 3 contains 2 quarter notes and 4 eighth notes, so you would play on 1 and 2, and then the eighth notes on 3 AN 4 AN. Measure 4 contains 4 eighth notes, followed by a half note, so you would play on 1 AN 2 AN 3, and nothing else, as the half note played on 3 fills the rest of the measure.

Measures 5 and 6 ⇨

In Measure 5 we have 8 eighth notes, so you would play on the counts of 1 AN 2 AN 3 AN 4 AN. Measure 6 you play the quarter note on 1, two eighths on 2 AN, two more on 3 AN, and a quarter note on 4.

Measures 7 and 8 ⇨

Measure 7, play quarter notes on 1 and 3, eighth notes on 2 AN and 4 AN. Measure 8 has quarter note rests on 1 and 3, so the only thing you will play is eighth notes and 2 AN and 4 AN.

Measures 9 and 10 ⇨

In measure 9 we see eighth note rests; we play on 1 AN 2, rest on AN, play on 3 AN 4, rest on AN. In measure 10 we now see a single eighth note; it looks like a quarter note but with a single flag waving to the right. We play 1 AN, rest on 2, play AN, then play the quarter notes on 3 and 4.

Measures 11 and 12 ⇨

And in measures 11 and 12 we have a mix of quarter notes and rests and eighth notes and rests.

Example 5 – Quarter and Eighth Notes, and Rests

1 AN 2 AN 3 AN 4 AN   1 AN 2 AN 3 AN 4 AN

1 AN 2 AN 3 AN 4 AN   1 AN 2 AN 3 AN 4 AN

1 AN 2 AN 3 AN 4 AN   1 AN 2 AN 3 AN 4 AN

1 AN 2 AN 3 AN 4 AN   1 AN 2 AN 3 AN 4 AN

1 AN 2 AN 3 AN 4 AN   1 AN 2 AN 3 AN 4 AN

1 AN 2 AN 3 AN 4 AN   1 AN 2 AN 3 AN 4 AN

Now let's add sixteenth notes, remembering of course that 4 sixteenth notes fit in the same space as either 1 quarter note, or two eighth notes. We'll count it as sixteenth notes:

1 E AN DA 2 E AN DA 3 E AN DA 4 E AN DA

Measures 1 and 2 ⇨

In Measure 1 you would play the quarter notes on 1 and 2, the eighth notes on 3 AN, and the sixteenth notes on 4 E AN DA. In Measure 2 you would play the quarter notes on 1 and 2, then sixteenth notes on 3 E AN DA 4 E AN DA. *Remember, even though you are not always playing sixteenth notes, you still want to count sixteenth notes, and play only those indicated in the music; this will help you properly space the notes so you are striking the quarter and eighth notes at the right time.*

Measures 3 and 4 ⇨

In Measure 3 you play the 1, but not the E AN DA, then play the 2 E AN DA 3 E AN DA 4 E AN DA. Measure 4, again the 1, but not the E AN DA, followed by 2 E AN DA; and the same pattern repeats for the 3 and 4.

Measures 5 and 6 ⇨

In Measure 5 we've mixed in some eighth notes. Measure 6 will help you understand why it is important to count in sixteenth notes, even though you are not always playing them. The measure does not start on the 1, as have all the other measures so far; this measure starts on the AN. How do you know when to play the AN? Easy, provided you count it as sixteenths. So you start your count as always, 1 E **AN** , and you play as soon as you get to the AN. So what you will play in this measure is (in bold):

1 E **AN** DA **2 E AN DA** 3 E **AN** DA **4 E AN DA**

Measures 7 and 8 ⇨

In Measure 7 we have two sixteenth notes (as we know from the two beams above each note) followed by an eighth note (as we know from the one beam), so we play on the 1 E AN, and the 2, and we repeat the same pattern in the rest of the measure. In Measure 8 we start with a eighth note, then two sixteenths, so we play:

1 E AN DA 2 E AN DA **3** E **AN DA 4** E AN DA

Measures 9 and 10 ⇨

In Measures 9 and 10 we put together these patterns, but we still count them as sixteenths so we get our spacing right:

1 E AN DA 2 E AN DA **3** E AN DA **4** E AN DA **1** E **AN DA 2 E AN** DA **3 E AN DA 4 E AN** DA

Please note—on this page, and throughout the remainder of the book, you will see certain "figures" (patterns) that you will encounter over and over in musical scores. While initially you will count these figures as we are showing you, you will ultimately become so familiar with each figure that you will simply recognize it—much as you see "dog", not "d" "o" "g", when you read the word "dog".

Example 6 – Sixteenth Notes

Now we know that to properly space our notes within each measure we need to count them as sixteenth notes, so let's try to read and play some measures that contain all the notes and rests we have seen so far.

We have labeled the notes and rests, but to get the spacing correct, count everything out loud as sixteenth notes:

1 E AN DA 2 E AN DA 3 E AN DA 4 E AN DA

Example 7
Whole, Half, Quarter, Eighth and Sixteenth Notes

Triplets

Triplets are just what they sound like, threes.

But the interesting thing with triplets is that they are 3 notes, but they are played in the same space you would normally play 2 notes! What this means is that for an "eighth note triplet" you would play 3 evenly spaced notes in the same space that you would normally play 2 eighth notes.

So instead of playing eighth notes as in Measure 1,   1   AN   2   AN   3   AN   4   AN
        you would play triplets as in Measure 2,   1 AN DA 2 AN DA 3 AN DA 4 AN DA
Triplets are *always* indicated by overhead bracketing and a small "3".

There are many ways to count triplets, and some people are more comfortable with one way or another. Some of the ways to count triplets are:

1 AN DA	2 AN DA	3 AN DA	4 AN DA
1 TRIP LET	2 TRIP LET	3 TRIP LET	4 TRIP LET
1 2 3	2 2 3	3 2 3	4 2 3
1 TA TA	2 TA TA	3 TA TA	4 TA TA

The thing that is a little challenging about triplets is that they occur within the course of music, so they are right there in the middle of quarter notes, eighth notes etc. Which means you will be doing your normal counting, probably in sixteenths, then you must immediately switch to a triplet count. For instance, in Measure 5 you will be counting 1 E AN DA, then a triplet—so the way to count Measure 5 is: **1** E **AN** DA **2 AN DA 3** E **AN** DA **4 AN DA**

While it might be a little confusing at first, it really is necessary to count your other notes in sixteenths to maintain proper spacing of notes. As you can see in Measures 7 through 10, there can be many combinations of 3 notes. Though there are many occasions that you may have a 3 note combination, the triplet is unique—it will always be counted as 3 notes evenly spaced, in the same space that would normally hold two notes.

There are also quarter note triplets and sixteenth note triplets, which we will cover in a later chapter.

Example 8 – Eighth Note Triplets

Rolls

We all know the sound of a drum roll, that exciting buzz that builds and builds as they light the fuse and, BOOM, ends as they shoot the man out of the cannon. Yes, we all know the sound of the "buzz roll" (which goes on and on), but most rolls are a specific number of beats, and a played in a specific way.

Let's look at a "5 Stroke Roll". In Measures 1 and 2 we see the 5 Stroke Roll is two Lefts, followed by two Rights, then a Left. And we would count it as:

"1 AN 2 AN 3(rests)" "1 AN 2 AN 3(rests)"

But we also see something new, we see a little "arrow" (>) over the "3's". This arrow indicates an "accent", which means that particular note is accented, played louder, than the other notes.

You will also notice you begin Measure 1 with the left stick, but you begin Measure 2 with the right stick. The need to accent, then alternate the beginning strokes, means the "sticking" (which stick you play with) is critical. Though this book is really about reading music, not about technique, we will show you exactly how to play the roll.

Measures 3 and 4 show the necessary sticking. The first stroke is a left tap, followed by a left upstroke (for an upstroke, you tap, then lift the stick to an up position), then a right tap, another right tap, and finally an accented left downstroke (for a downstroke, you strike from the up position, and after striking keep the stick down near the surface, ready for the next tap). The lifting of the stick on the upstroke is critical, as this puts the stick in position to play the accented downstroke; the downstroke brings the stick back to correct starting position for the next roll.

In Measures 5 and 6 you see the roll in sixteenth notes, which you would count as:

1 E AN DA <u>2</u>   3 E AN DA <u>4</u>

In Measure 7 we speed up to 32nd notes, which would be counted:

1 E <u>AN</u> 2 E <u>AN</u> 3 E <u>AN</u> 4 E <u>AN</u>

In this example however, on the 1's and the E 's, and the 3's and the E's, you play a double strokes—on the AN's you play the accented downstroke.

The examples above illustrate the way the roll is *played*, not the way the roll is *written*. The way you will see a 5 Stroke Roll written in a musical score is shown in Measure 8. It looks like two eighth notes connected by a beam on top and a bow underneath, with a 5 over the first note, and two slashes across the first note. It may, or may not, have an accent on the final note.

Measures 9 through 12 are some examples of 5 Stroke Rolls amidst other notes.

Example 9 – The 5 Stroke Roll

We showed you the 5 stroke roll on the prior page, and here are the 7, 9, 10, 11, 13 and 15 stroke rolls. The left part of each line shows you how the roll is played[4]; the right part of each line shows you how the roll will be written in a piece of music.

There are as many lengths of drum rolls as you can imagine, but the 5, 7, 9, 10, 11, 13 and 15 stroke rolls are all elements of the 26 Original Rudiments of Drumming[5]. The remaining rudiments are various flams, ruff, drags, ratamacues and paradiddles. We encourage you to study and master the rudiments, as they will prove invaluable to you regardless what type of drumming you pursue.

---

[4] Please note that on the 7 and 9 stroke rolls we are showing you the rolls starting with both the left and right hands. On the 10, 11, 13 and 15 stroke rolls we show only starting with the left hand; the rolls are to be played right-handed as well.

[5] For the proper form and technique for various rolls, the Original Rudiments of Drumming, and various other drumming techniques, please visit our website, www.drummerSS.com, or check out our other publications.

Example 10 – More Rolls

31

Other Kinds of "Rests"

You are familiar with "rests" from our earlier pages showing notes and rests. There are really just two choices with drum music—you play a note, or you rest. Unfortunately, there are not just two choices when it comes to playing, or resting; there are a couple other forms of notation with which you should be familiar.

Measures 1 and 2 ⇨
> First we have our basic rests—whole, half, quarter, eighth, etc.—which we've shown you before, as in Measures 1 and 2.

Measures 3 through 6 ⇨
> Another method is the curved "bow" which extends from the bottom of one note, to the bottom of the next note. What this tells you to do is to *play the first note* (where the bow starts), *but don't play the second note* (where the bow ends). Any kind of notes can be involved, and any and all combinations are possible. See measures 3 through 6—and please note that *Measures 3 and 4 are played exactly like Measures 1 and 2*, it is just written in a different way.

Measures 7 through 10 ⇨
> Yet another method, shown in Measures 7 through 10, is by placing a dot immediately after a note. (This is not technically a "rest" but it has the same effect.) When there is a dot placed after a note, it increases the *value* of the note by half. For example, a dot placed after a quarter note increases the value of that note to a quarter note *plus* an eighth note. A dot placed after an eighth note increases the value of that note to and eighth note *plus* a sixteenth note. Which means if the dot follows a quarter note, you don't play again for the duration of a quarter note *plus* an eighth note. A dot could follow any note, and the same formula would apply (a dot could even follow a rest as shown in Measure 9).

> In Measures 7 and 8 we see a quarter note followed by a dot, which means the value of the quarter note is now 1/4 + 1/8, or 3/8—so that dotted quarter note will now take up the same space as three eighth notes. In Measure 9 we see a quarter note rest followed by a dot—so that dotted quarter note rest will now take up the same space as three eighth note rests. And in Measure 10 we see an eighth note followed by a dot, so the value of that eighth note is now 1/8 + 1/16, or 3/16—so that dotted eighth note will now take up the same space as three sixteenth notes. Sounds complicated, eh? Not really so—when you see it written in music it will be very obvious to you what is to be played.

All that said, the most likely way you will see rests written is the fundamental way which we showed you earlier, in Example 2 (page 13).

Example 11 — Other Kinds of "Rests"

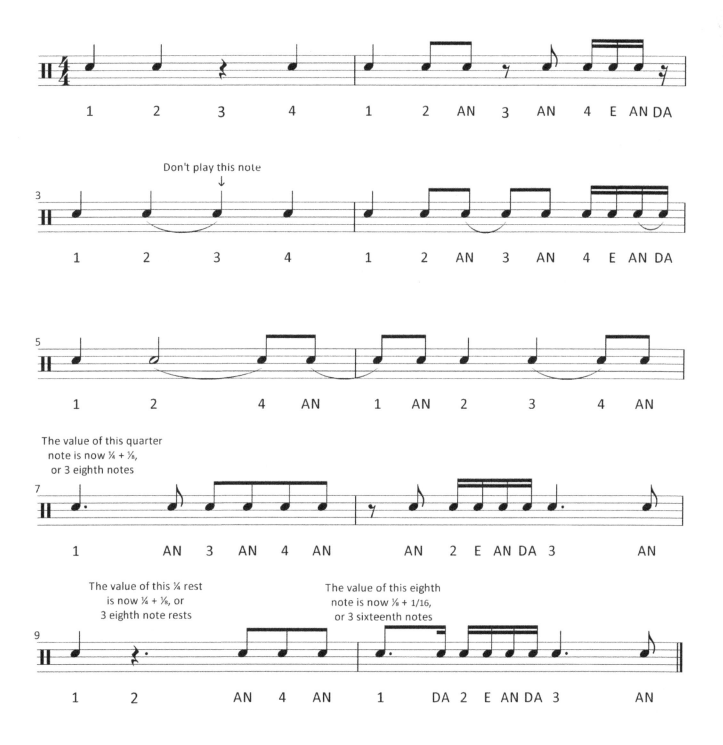

Other Kinds of Triplets

We already know that triplets are 3 notes, played in the same space that would normally take 2 notes. So that if we were playing eighth note triplets, instead of playing eighth notes (1 AN 2 AN etc.) we would play triplets (1 AN DA 2 AN DA etc.) Sixteenth note triplets are no different, except that we will play the triplet (3 evenly spaced notes) in the same space that would normally contain 2 sixteenth notes.

Let us look at Measure 1—on the 1st and 3rd beats we have 2 sixteenth notes, **1 E** AN 2 AN **3 E** AN 4 AN. Now let's look at the 2nd measure; exactly the same except where the sixteenth notes had been in Measure 1 we now have triplets. So where the sixteenth notes appeared, the 1 E and the 3 E, we will instead play three notes. But remember, we still need to fit those three notes in the same space so that the eighth note AN happens at the exact same time as it would have if it had been preceded by either two sixteenth notes or an eighth note.

The counting of these can be a little interesting. As we showed you earlier, we count our eighth note triplets 1 AN DA 2 AN DA etc.; so what we do is use that same kind of count for sixteenth note triplets.

So, we would count ♫♫ as 1 AN DA AN,

and we would count ♫♫ in Measure 6 as 2 e AN DA AN (of course, the "e" isn't played, it's a space).

There is no hard and fast rule for how to count sixteenth note triplets. Whatever way you choose, the three notes must be evenly spaced and must happen in the same space as would normally contain two sixteenth notes.

We suggest you to count these out loud, and practice them slowly; this will allow each of these triplet patterns to become engrained in both your head and your "muscle memory". When you are playing these at a decent tempo you will find it impossible to actually count each note; therefore repetitive practice at a slow tempo while counting, gradually building to a quicker tempo, will allow you to recognize each figure (combination of notes) and play that figure. As we said before, while initially you need to count these figures, you will ultimately become so familiar with each figure that you will simply recognize it—much like when you see the written word "music", you don't think "m" "u" "s" "i" "c"; you recognize and read the word "music".

Example 12 – Sixteenth Note Triplets

A quarter note triplet is 3 evenly spaced notes that are played in the space that would normally hold 2 quarter notes.

In Measure 1 we see eighth notes on the 3 and the 4, and in Measure 2 we see eighth note triplets.

In Measure 3 we see quarter notes on the 3 and the 4, and in Measure 4 we see quarter note triplets.

The interesting thing here, again, is how to count. Remember, *the three notes must be evenly spaced.* Take a look at Measure 2, and Measure 4, directly below it:

In Measure 2 we would count beats 3 and 4 as 3 AN DA 4 AN DA.

Measure 4 we would count *exactly the same way,* but we would only play on the counts we have put in bold type **3** an **DA** 4 **AN** da . By counting it and playing it this way, we get 3 notes evenly spaced where we would normally have two quarter notes.

Example 13 – Quarter Note Triplets

Thirty-second Notes

Now we'll look at thirty-second notes. There are 2 thirty-second notes in a sixteenth note, 4 thirty-seconds in an eighth note, 16 thirty-second notes in a quarter note, or 32 thirty-second notes in a whole note.

With all the notes we've learned so far, we have counted *each* note as it is played. While this method would theoretically work for 32nd notes, in practice it just doesn't work. When playing at any normal tempo it becomes impossible to verbally (or even mentally) count each 32nd—there are just too many of them to verbalize as quickly as you would need.

So the answer is simple—we count 32^{nds} the same way we would count sixteenth notes: 1 E A DA 2 E AN DA etc., *but,* wherever a 32nd note, or a string of 32nd notes, occurs we play 2 notes in the space that would have taken one sixteenth note.

So in the second measure on the next page we play our eighth notes 1 AN, then our sixteenths, 2 E AN DA, then our eighths 3 AN, then our sixteenths followed by a 32nd, counting 4 E AN DA, but playing 4 E AN DADA.

You might try to verbalize the actual count if you want, but we think you will find it becomes quite a tongue twister, and you may have more trouble counting the notes than playing them. So just count as sixteenths but play two notes every time 32^{nds} are indicated.

Example 14 – Thirty-second Notes

Putting It All Together—Adding Your Instruments

Now we'll add multiple instruments to the staff, using the snare drum, bass drum, closed hi-hat played with stick, and the hi-hat played with the foot pedal. Page 9 shows you the staff, and where each instrument appears on it. You will find this easier to play if you *count out loud.*

Measures 1 and 2 ⇨

    In Measures 1 and 2 we will play on the top hi-hat with our stick, on the eighth notes, 1 AN 2 AN 3 AN 4 AN. We will keep the hi-hat closed by keeping our foot down on the pedal, so we will get a tic sound as we strike the hi-hat with our stick.

Measures 3 and 4 ⇨

    Now we add the bass drum on the 1s and 3s, and on each of the ANs that precede the 1s and 3s, while continuing to play the hi-hat on the eighth notes.

Measures 5 and 6 ⇨

    We add the hi-hat, played with our foot, on the 2 and 4.

Measures 7 through 10 ⇨

    And finally in Measures 7 and 8 we add the snare drum.

Take your time and play it slowly. Since everything is played on the eighth notes, you can count it all as eighth notes, adding each instrument as you go, while continuing to play the instruments from the lines before. So start Measure 1 playing on the closed hi-hat with your stick, then add in the bass, then the hi-hat with your foot, and finally the snare—and when you get to the end you'll be playing the Latin rhythm known as the Bossa Nova.

Example 15 – Adding Your Instruments

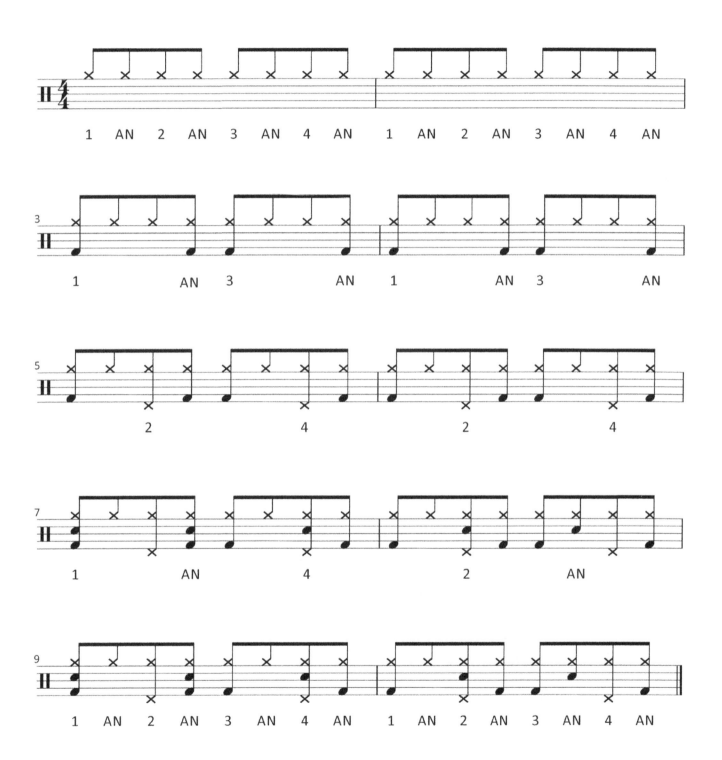

Dynamics

The dynamics of a piece of music refers to the volume at which it is played. Written music will contain notation regarding the volume, and the relative volume of individual notes.

Measures 1 and 2 ⇨

As we saw in our 5 Stroke Roll example, a little "arrow" over a note indicates that note is "accented", or played louder than the other notes. Again in Measures 1 and 2 we see our 5 Stroke Roll.

Measures 3 and 4 ⇨

In Measures 3 and 4 we see one of the Rudiments of drumming, the paradiddle[6]; and you will notice the first stroke of each paradiddle is accented. As in the 5 Stroke Roll, the "sticking" is crucial. The second stroke of each paradiddle is an "upstroke"; this upstroke puts your stick in the correct position for what will be the next stroke with that stick, which will be the accented downstroke of the next paradiddle.

Measures 5 and 6 ⇨

You also may see symbols instructing you to play more loudly (forte), or more softly (piano). In Measure 5 we see the symbol for "crescendo" over the measure; for crescendo you play continually more loudly for the duration of the crescendo. In Measure 6 we see the symbol for "diminuendo"; for diminuendo you play continually more softly for the duration of the diminuendo.

Measures 7 through 10 ⇨

In Measures 7 and 8 we see the Bossa Nova again; but in Measures 9 and 10 we see it modified, with what look like parentheses around some of the bass drum notes. Parentheses around a note, any note, turn it into a "ghost note". A ghost note is the opposite of an accented note – a ghost note is to be played very softly, lightly, weakly . . . barely audible.

The use of dynamics, playing certain notes or phrases more loudly or softly, has a dramatic effect on the sound and the feel of the music. You will notice the difference between the Bossa Nova as originally written with all bass notes played strongly, and as written in Measures 9 and 10, is really quite dramatic.

---

[6] The paradiddle is one of the rudiments of drumming. For the proper form and technique for the Original Rudiments of Drumming, plus other essentials to developing a strong foundation, please visit our website, www.drummerSS.com, or check out our other publications.

Example 16 – Dynamics

R R L L R   L L R R L   RRLLR   LLRRL   RRLLR   LLRRL

DOWN UP TAP TAP DOWN UP TAP TAP
R   L   R   R   L   L   R   L   R L R R L R L L R L R R L R L L

For the video, go to our website,
www.drummerSS.com

43

Where to Start, Where to End, What to Repeat

Measures 1 through 4 ⇨

At the beginning of the first measure of a piece of music you will see the "time signature". At the end of the last measure you will see a vertical double line.

Some pieces are broken up into sections; section beginnings are noted by a double vertical line followed by a colon, and section ends are noted by a double vertical line preceded by a colon. There are many reasons a piece of music may be broken into sections. For instance, some songs have refrains, and may require you to play differently for each verse . . . however, you may be required to play the identical same notes for the refrains. The music will be notated, and numbered, in such a way that you will be able to distinguish each verse, and the refrain; the notation will guide you as to what order to play each section. (There are so many potential variants of this that we are not including examples.)

Measures 5 through 10 ⇨

There are many circumstances that require a drummer to play the same pattern, over and over; this is when you will see the "repeat" symbol, which tells you to repeat the prior measure. Sometimes this might require just the snare, or perhaps the snare, hi-hat and bass, or some other combination—whatever combination of notes and instruments appear in the prior measure are what is to be repeated.

Measures 5 and 6 show the Mozambique, a Latin rhythm. To get the right sound you play the left and right hands on different instruments. Try the right stick on the metal edge of the snare, or on a cowbell, and try the left on the snare drum. (Try other combinations, too.) Play the bass notes on the bass drum.

First we play Measures 5, 6, 7 and 8. Then Measure 9 has a "repeat" symbol, as does Measure 10—so in Measure 9 we repeat Measure 8, and in Measure 10 we repeat Measure 9.

Example 17 – Beginning, End, Repeat

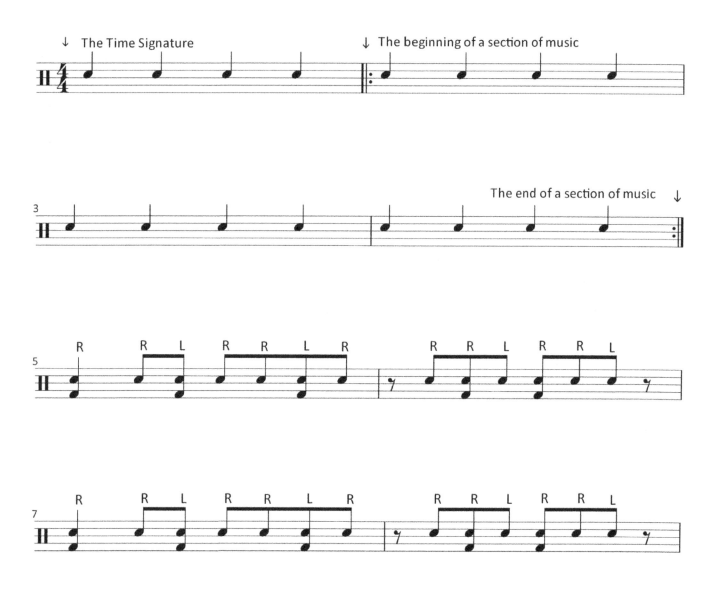

Other Symbols, Note Heads, Articulations

There are many symbols you may see in written music. On the next page are some that you may encounter.

Hi-hat, Open or Closed—when playing hi-hat with your stick, it is assumed the hi-hat is closed, unless you see a little "o" over the note which indicates to leave it open. When playing hi-hat with your foot it is assumed you close it all the way in the normal manner; however, if you see a little "o" over (or under) the note, that indicates you play a foot splash.

More cymbals—We already know (from page 9) where our crash, hi-hat and ride cymbals appear. There could be more cymbals; a splash cymbal is usually shown on the first line above the staff, and a China cymbal is shown on the second line above the staff.

Choked cymbals—when the composer wants you to "choke" the cymbal (grab it to stop the tone) immediately after striking it, an apostrophe will be used right after the cymbal note.

Rim Shot—a "rim shot" is played by striking both the drum head and the rim simultaneously. It is indicated by a slash though the note head.

Cross Stick—cross stick is played by laying the stick the across the drumhead, with the barrel of the stick up over the rim. The part of the stick that is lying on the rim is raised and used to strike the rim. This is indicated by a circle with a slash surrounding the note head.

Triangle—A triangle appears on the first line above the staff; the note head will be in the shape of a triangle. A "muted" triangle (one that you are grabbing with your hand to prevent the ringing sound) triangle will be indicated by a "+" over the note.

Cowbell—Also indicated by a triangle note head, the cowbell will appear in the top space of the staff. Like a triangle, a muted cowbell will be indicated with a "+" over the note.

Woodblocks—Woodblocks are also indicated by a triangular note head, and will appear in the upper section of the staff. The higher line is for the highest pitch.

Gong—a gong appears as a triangle note head on the bottom line of the staff.

Stem up, or stem down—you will see notes with the stems pointed up, and with stems pointed down. The direction the stem is pointing makes no difference; it is the note head, and where it is placed on the staff that determines what instrument and what note you play. Stems may be pointed up or down; there is no hard and fast rule for this. Sometimes the composer will point the stems for the hand parts up, and for the foot parts down, but this is not always the case.

Unique symbols—in addition to "standardized" symbols, a composer may well create a symbol or use a symbol in a unique way; if this is the case, it will be explained in either a key or text preceding the music.

Example 18 – Other Symbols

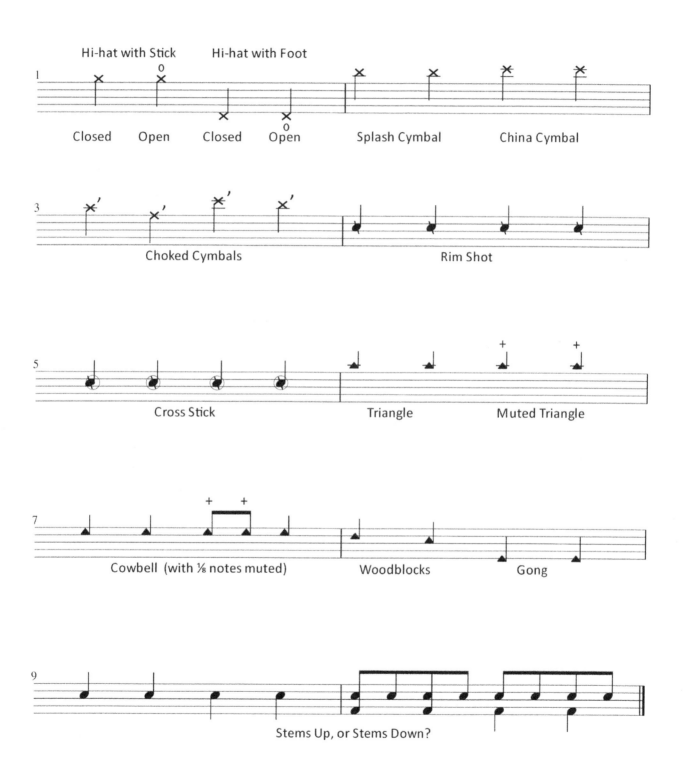

You Can Read!

OK, you may be thinking, can I really read drum music? Take a look at the next page; your first thought is probably "Omigosh, I could never read *that!*" WRONG—*you can read it!*

What you're looking at is a band arrangement, an arrangement for many instruments, and for lyrics. Reading the "Voice" line, you will surely recognize the tune.

Toward the bottom is the Percussion music. What do you see?

- The first thing is, as always, the time signature—which in this case is 2/4.
    - So you know that in each measure there will be 2 beats and each will be a quarter note (or any combination of notes that equals a quarter note).
    - Since it's 2/4, you know the way to count it is:
        1 E AN DA 2 E AN DA 1 E AN DA 2 E AN DA

- Then look where the notes are placed on the staff:
    - We see notes on the snare drum line.
    - Down lower, we see notes on the bass drum line.

- Then we read the notes:
    - The snare drum is played on the 1---AN DA 2, in each of the first two measures. In the third measure it is played on the 1---AN DA 2---AN DA.
    - The bass drum is played on the "1" in each measure.
    - And so on.

While some pieces of music may look scary on paper, remember, drum music is all about what instrument you strike, and when. So as long as you know the time signature, which drum or cymbal is to be played, and what each note, rest, accent, etc. looks like, then you *can* read the music.

Don't be intimidated when you look at written music. You now know the basics of reading percussion music, and with this knowledge you'll be able to read and figure out any piece of drum music.

Example 19 – Yankee Doodle

Composition: Richard Shuckburg
Arrangement: Chad Criswell

Yank-ee Doo-dle went to to-wn ri-ding on a po — ny Stuck a fea-ther in his cap and called it mac-a — ro — ni

Arrangement courtesy of Chad Criswell and MusicEdMagic.com

49

About the Authors

Stu Segal grew up in a house filled with music. Though not musicians, his parents were always playing Broadway Show tunes, Harry Belafonte, Bobby Darin, Mario Lanza, and Al Jolson. When Stu was six he heard the hound dog man for the first time, and his foot has been tapping ever since.

Stu had a long career in banking, and later as the owner of motorcycle stores. At over 60, he began to pursue his long-forgotten childhood study of drums, which led to re-learning how to read music, hence the writing of this book.

Stu lives just outside New York City. He rides motorcycles, juggles balls, clubs & knives, listens to rock 'n roll and New Orleans jazz, and plays drums. You can find him annually at the World Science Fiction Convention, the Westminster Kennel Club Show, various rock concerts and motorcycle events, on the internet, and occasionally in the French Quarter. He is hard at work on his next book with Jimmy; you can follow their progress at www.drummerSS.com

Jimmy Sica has been drumming on things since he was a little kid; before his parents got him sticks he used the wood rods from old-fashioned clothing hangers. Originally self-taught, Jimmy began drumming professionally at age 16, and has been working as an entertainer ever since.

Jimmy earned an undergraduate degree in music, and later graduated the American Musical and Dramatic Academy, College and Conservatory of the Performing Arts, in New York City. AMDA, which was founded by Philip Burton (step-father of the great British actor Richard Burton), gave Jimmy the knowledge, training and discipline to develop into a well-rounded performer—musician, actor, singer, dancer.

Jimmy has played drums with The Drifters, Screamin' Jay Hawkins, Johnny Maestro and many more; he has been a pit drummer for shows like Chicago, Pippin and Jesus Christ Superstar. He has acted on both stage and screen. For many years he organized and managed his own band.

In the late 1990s Jimmy began teaching drums to aspiring students (he has, of course, also taught them to read music). He continues to play professionally, is working on his next book, and continues to teach drumming to select students.

For more information about books, personal instruction, or to contact Stu or Jimmy, please visit our website, www.drummerSS.com

---

Do us a favor, please!
If you enjoyed our book, if it taught you to read drum music, gave you a better understanding of written music, taught you about time signatures, please help us get the book out to others. Please go to amazon.com and rate our book! It'll just take a minute.
Thank you!

Made in the USA
Monee, IL
02 September 2020